How To Find All Missing Persons / Unsolved Cases. And Collect All Reward Offers. Volume XXXX. THE CASE OF PAULINE SOWRY

DAVID GOMADZA

www.twofuture.world

How To Find All Missing Persons / Unsolved Cases. And
Collect All Reward Offers. Volume XXXX. THE CASE OF PAULINE SOWRY

Copyright © 2024 David Gomadza

All rights reserved.

Paperback ISBN: 9798328648172

How To Find All Missing Persons / Unsolved Cases. And
Collect All Reward Offers. Volume XXXX. THE CASE OF PAULINE SOWRY

DEDICATION

To a better future.

How To Find All Missing Persons / Unsolved Cases. And
Collect All Reward Offers. Volume XXXX. THE CASE OF PAULINE SOWRY

How To Find All Missing Persons / Unsolved Cases. And
Collect All Reward Offers. Volume XXXX. THE CASE OF PAULINE SOWRY

CONTENTS

How To Find All Missing Persons /
Unsolved Cases.
And Collect All Reward Offers. Volume XXXX.
THE CASE OF PAULINE SOWRY 1
Afterlife Conversation.

and The Court Of Creation.   5

The Killers.   20

How To Find All Missing Persons / Unsolved Cases. And
Collect All Reward Offers. Volume XXXX. THE CASE OF PAULINE SOWRY

How To Find All Missing Persons / Unsolved Cases. And
Collect All Reward Offers. Volume XXXX. THE CASE OF PAULINE SOWRY

ACKNOWLEDGMENTS

Tomorrow's World Order

How To Find All Missing Persons / Unsolved Cases. And
Collect All Reward Offers. Volume XXXX. THE CASE OF PAULINE SOWRY

How To Find All Missing Persons / Unsolved Cases. And Collect All Reward Offers. Volume XXXX. THE CASE OF PAULINE SOWRY

BACKGROUND INFORMATION

nsw police offer $500k reward in bid to solve cold case of missing mum pauline sowry
new south wales police are optimistic a $500,000 reward could solve the mystery what happened to wollongong woman pauline sowry more than 30 years ago.

the "kind, caring and loving" woman was last seen by her family in december 1993 in the northern suburbs of wollongong.

ms sowry was declared deceased by the coroner in 2008.

no-one has ever been charged in relation to her disappearance or death and her body has not been found.

today the state government announced that $500,000 would be awarded to anyone with information that leads to a conviction in the case.
Son's tearful plea

Thirty years after he last saw her, discussing his mother still brings Jason Lawrence to tears.

"My mother was a kind, caring and a loving mother," he said at a press conference in Wollongong this morning.

"I believe someone has taken advantage of her kindness and vulnerability, so my family and I plead with the public to come forward with any information or knowledge of her disappearance."

Mr Lawrence was flanked by Ms Sowry's sisters, Jill Sowry and Michelle Jones, as well as her brother, Simon Sowry, as he made the impassioned plea for information.

The family held images of Ms Sowry and each wiped away tears as her son spoke of the impact her disappearance had on the family

How To Find All Missing Persons / Unsolved Cases. And
Collect All Reward Offers. Volume XXXX. THE CASE OF PAULINE SOWRY

TOMORROW'S WORLD ORDER'S PERSPECTIVES

USE OF PREDEFINED AFTERLIFE PARAMETERS

These guide souls the moment it exist the human body on its journey to Yahweh the creator these define what to do and what to expect as you go to hell or heaven if a souk leaves earth it enters ozone orbit and instantly everything reboots for it to start a new phase of life after living the earth's body now what happens is that it enters the ozone orbit and a simply click caused by the sudden drop of pressure from -1186 to – 20 means the bottom shaft of the soul will lift rapidly and this pushes its back into the air higher than its head best example is a penguin but with real human legs and head just the shape now God created a life predefined program for them instead of asking what should I do and where should I go they instantly know from predefined stencils if you did well and talked most about God then heaven is for you if you did evil and talked more about the devil then the devil is yours now if we Ask what can be of humans without souks this is the answer dead forever your soul is you a new transformation to the electromagnetic waves life where you see Yahweh for the first time and praise him and wish you had seen him a long time ago because of his Majesty and will always be there forever now what are all these you may ask these are rules to be guided by in the creation court in short it has everything humans know about the judges and the presiding judge who will always be Yahweh and 84 angels surrounding the altar 28 high priests who always say Yahweh have mercy on humans and 74 smaller courts priests who always say Yahweh has mercy on humans and 96 princesses who say glory to Yahweh forever and ever amen we have 96 elders who always say if I can why he can't meaning if the devil can drink blood why can't Yahweh who created the devil and blood do the same now this is not the same as saying if the devil can kill why can Yahweh its more on professional grounds rather than challenging now if we look at the inside of the court we have 81 priests surrounding the altar who say Yahweh be merciful to humans but if they disobey you we put hem on trial for you and kill them for

you almighty Yahweh inside this is a round circle where Yahweh sits and asks questions now if we look deep inside the court you will see that there are other things that resemble earth high courts like benches and chairs 10 times human sizes for the gods who are so enormous 2 are equal to 84 billion humans in size
predefined parameters for humans after death as in know what is inside is a large size of books the book of creation is among them with 10897867892836789012348678901245861789011 pages and is divided into humans first then chapter for animals then a chapter for angles then a chapter for gods and a chapter for Joseph Yahweh's best friend and a chapter for Yahweh's best friend's wife Anna and a chapter for Yahweh's wife Catitighit and lastly a chapter for Yahweh and recently a chapter for davidgomadza as Yahweh's representative on earth marking the new beginnings starting in 2025

1. tell us who killed you
2. tell us what killed you
3. tell us why and who killed you
4. tell us why you died
5. tell us what could have been done and is not done
6. tell us what could be and why
7. tell is when this happened
8. tell us why this is so
9. tell us why this is so
10. what can be done to improve this

What does the book of creation say about davidgomadza David Gomadza is the first and last ruler to be appointed by Yahweh fir the next 25 billion years and will act as his representative on earth deciding cases and upholding his principles on earth and as such has been entitled to 489 trillion dollars in assets this number signifies eternity among humans and the beginning of a new Era chapter 7867892802893862841890287689018320867890123486789018236487289128610 Creation manual the new Era of new electromagnetic wave conduit signed and dated by Yahweh himself on 27may2024 at 237800 Yatime
creation.universe.ya.start.end.find.davidgomadza.ya.askya.ya

Ask.read.creation.manucreation.universe.ya.start.end.find.davidgoma askya.ya

Ask.rulesofthecourt.start.now.start
David Gomadza welcome the rules of court are guiding principles that tell you what to do and how to do it first you must always say I believe in the court of creation and I shall abide by he rules of this court and shall always do things according to the rules of this court in deciding the cases I am assigned to you must ask what can be done so that you know all your options before making choices the court system will make it easy to check files and ask the outcomes of the decision ask the court the final decision in any case.

THE AFTERLIFE CONVERSATION AND THE COUNCIL OF CREATION'S ANAYLSIS.

IMPORTANT!!
READ ALL BOOK FIRST UNTIL THE END BEFORE MAKING UP YOUR MIND

i was killed by my own son he said mum what for dinner and i said nothing but food he laughed and said what else could be for dinner between a mum and a son and i said just food mum son right why you ask he said i get aroused but and stopped i laughed and said if your father was here then what he said i can be him no one can love you the way i do for a thousand days and i said why days and not years he said that what i got left to give after that i move out of your house i become a man then start and he said i can if you can but not come back again but and stopped and i said aren't you my favorite son if you can't come back then what if i fall sick who will look after me and he said i can come to you and i said no we can't stay here forever i don't want to lose you over sex with my own my god that would be like hell on wheels so he left and i cried all night and slept now he feels embarrassed and moved out abruptly then never come back until i called the police and said he is missing that's the mistake i did because he started ringing just to say i am okay then he stopped again then this time i find him girlfriend my niece who he always said she is hot and they get on well until he said i let her go the sex is boring i get nothing with her and cried then hugged me and i realised what that meant and i called her to come so she knocked the door while he was crying and i said why you made him cry and he said maybe he wants mum's vagina because he call me your name then i reslised that he acting like his father that's what he used to do before he die so he said okay i marry you then so we keep the house secure okay and left and for days i did not know what was going then i said what about the house he said the police said the house is for sale because next month your mother with her cheating boyfriend are broke fantasying about sex with son and forgot the one paying the bills and i froze because he had started acting strangely just phoning and saying i am okay then he said i found someone young too who make me wonder what life is all about and took his clothes and left then i sat down and said what can be of houses without mother's then i heard a message that said after two weeks you will fail to pay the house where would you get the money to pay the bills i sat down and got goosebumps and cursed i realised that i needed joe more so i said come back to me at least settle these bills then i start looking for money then he said what can be of sons without mother's it said great in fact that release insurance money for him and i said eat can be of us together and it only said death now because the police are now involved because you said he wants sex with you as a son when no one to pay bills we see problems so we take over the house to protect capital gains tax so i got really upset i smashed the tv and it broke into pieces that when he came he only said what we do now that you are finally single i can explain i could see the frustration in his eyes that i tried to remind you o dad and know why he left and why you are better with him so he keep paying the house bills and i felt like an idiot and sat down now i felt getting really aroused around him so i said if you want we can but for 200 dollars and he puffed the tea in his mouth and went to throw up so hard that i threw up hard as well then went in there and cleaned up and said i didn't mean it and he slapped me and said it hurts you screwing that fool for 100 a night when i can double it after all and i cut in and said he is not related to me so no laws broken and he thought hard and said what laws and i said to protect kids then he said this is what this is about and i said yes with you it's mother failure so he sat down and cursed and said who broke the television and i said i did but can replace it he said who broke the house i said i can fix it and he said who broke everything and i kept quiet and he said why you don't confess so i say you break everything even all these rules but that was a lie do i refused i said if you had not raised the issue then no one would have said anything so whose fault so he cried and said i only said it to help you see what he needs as a man daily sex or he walk away i am son not for sex but big love okay because you think of me for sex i strangle you and now call the police because i ran away and you called them now i don't have peace with them they activated an aty to keep an eye on me because of you but i understand you prefer me to be labeled as a mother rapist but i was helping you so you pay bills and i cried realizing the graveness of the accusation and my heart skipped a bit and he said i feel rage around you the woman i loved the most betrayed me and i have no one my girlfriend walked out your niece abandoned me and i nearly killed myself the other night but i pray for a better day then i cried and said it's all lies i only said that you run away nothing to do with sex so i refused to be blamed for your failures he said you are my mother to love me is to protect me this is just making me made not to work so how would you pay bills mother some of the things are not just right they take the house from us then we will lose and he cried himself to sleep so i went to police and said clear my son so that i work and he work they said it's precautionary only he can work so he left and never saw him again for 2 years then one night i went back with aly and he came in the middle of the night and simply went in his room and slept deep sleep that now i said when around him let's be there so he know we are together again as his wish then he woke up as we started fondling and he said okay i get the picture you guys you are back together i am proud of you two i love you deeply i am myself back again i felt really strong love goodnight and he slept and things got back together again ever since he never worry or run away then we stayed another two years and aly died in a car accident and he work up in the middle of the night and strangled me in sleep and called the police and said i was about to go out when aly said call the police and ran out i went in to check but she was already dead he killed her find him right now then he went to sleep then the next morning he was involved in a car crash that killed 8 other people while running away from killing his mother so he said i want my mother back how i pay bills then he sold the house and left as i know now from the court of creation deliberations.

died on 22 december 1993 killed by her own son astertey who said what can i do to keep the house and his own aty for the first time said kill mother then keep the house her life insurance will pay the bills fir 85 years exactly for you to die peacefully when he used his aty which he said was a gift from Yahweh wrote a master plan where he would his mother but first he must take out aly once and for all this is what he did according to his aty

1. break the valve to the breaks
2. if he asks say ok everything so he don't check
3. if he smile you frown
4. if he swerve put the breaks
5. if he looks on then you look down
6. if he sits you stand
7. if he stand you sit
8. if he ask then say okay
9. if he say how then you say why
10. if he open the door then be done
11. if he say hey say hie
12. if he say who then you say why
13. if he ask then you ignore
14. if he say why then say who
15. if he say hello then say hie
16. if he say why then you say how
17. if he say understand then you say who why
18. if he say if then say what
19. who is what and why
20. hey if you then what

he rolled the car first and instantly slapped on the breaks that they locked then pushed in the car and started it then pushed it back he then said hey aty what is you then it said a disguised policeman then his heart flipped then said a dirty one right because this is banned under the Australian laws and it said yes but then he said why you don't listen i said a dirty one it exited now he is in his car and said what can be of stepfather who hide from his step son now what is of him if he can't be there he then smiled and said i can if he can but then and said what could be of mother's who can't pay then he said they are like the dead living among the living and only a matter of time before things turn soar and he said if i can can she and he waited but what happened is that his aty sent a message to her mother's and asked her personally if i can die to save the house can you too then he said no again for her mother before she relied then that became her response so he planned to get him propose on false account so he set up questions he asks not linked to proposal so they are linked to proposal so he said can you not want to eat so he said i want to but then he said after such a long time i think you should know by yourself that you want so he said i want to okay maybe i ask your mother if she want too

then he said after all that time why would she refuse then he said i don't know maybe not just ready then he said ready she think she can be young again i don't think so time is flying enough and it's hell on earth so what can we do us he said i will see maybe we start preparation and he gets really excited and run and hugged him and said i love you but she die without your love and i love her very much so she is yours okay i give you and that was what made him angry that he just went to his car and jumped in and raved off for the first time and left his mother was now listening and she heard the car revving then checked who normally only her son raved the car so she said what is that all about and he said he tried to propose to you i said my mum not for sale go and find a prostitute so he got upset and left but i said that so he said i want to marry her but this jerk run away with a tail between his legs her mother said aty reply silently even i can't hear it so it plays everything and realized that he might feel cheated and kill himself she called him and now fearing what the police can end up saying she did not call there but said my husband is missing instead when they arrived they were not married but about to then he ran to prepare but her mother did not get that part and said i don't know on her part then a huge knock at the door startled her it was two hours after this she said who bloody knock like a hungry hyena and the police said we have bad knews your sin did not make it so the mother cried first and said who they said the other boy and she said okay my step son and took the message sat down and said what this is about how can killing him solve the problem he is already married and his wife gets everything are you stupid you can't read if you think that i am a part of this then think again i refuse because we gain nothing if he is dead that means we need him so he cursed and said so what is the other option? this silenced her instantly and all realised missed opportunities and had instantly fell asleep now exhausted and said god forgive me if i don't listen to you bye mum you keep protecting all option i think now i understand and strangled her once at night but so fast that she could not sent a message to ya her naked was broken that there was not even brain commands the court of creation returned a verdict of accidental death when she fell according

her long ago started at 20.28 pm and died at 20.32 pm at 85 stert street near baywhich she was buried at cemetery 08928367890184678903867890286789028486789012480

god i got killed by my own son asoretp who said what can be of mother's who can't afford to pat then strangled me in my sleep at 20.28pm i know because he sent me a text message that said what can you do to save the house when asked what makes you think that it was your sun she only said that she knew because of the text message but deep

god i died i was killed by my own son he said what can be of mother's who can pay then strangled me and cried saying mum sorry mum but who pay rent if i die you still struggle but if you die then i can pay so you go i stay but i really loved you but you go to daddy i can handle things now mum then i heard him throw things on me just before i die

i am stert a hired killer the son said i can if you can but you can then better because life will still remain harder so i said i can help i can help so he asked how then i said i can break her neck then you finish her off by smoothing for good sending off he said i can't and i said okay i can do everything and he said okay so i sent ten codes to her

1. 286878902348790
2. 786898789234890124890
3. 778678902867890284890

4. 28678902867890283678290
5. 23456780386789028490230
6. 789068483867890284123
7. 7892867890483867890
8. 77283867890284867890
9. 228877886809876084321
10. 334890284567892853210
code 1 breaks the neck
code 2 stops the breaking
code 3 asks for long ago which
breathing silent non detected
ast 0 no will power to fight
aso 7
as8 3
as1 2
as3 9
as4 8
as6 9
ass 2
asks 6
asss0 10 measures endurance and stamina
as3 6
as8 9
as18 3
as20 10
as6 17
as8 9
as12 4
as18 24
as10 9
as14 16
assist 2
asseto 7
assad 16
all this reveal that before the strangulation she had no.medical condition she was in perfect health but who is stert this is a common name in these murder case stert is a computer periphery that is

attached and gives instructions that it executes in this case if it is executing the question is on behalf of you we can always read the first and last logs

first log i just got picked up at random to kill a one pauline sowry by what looks like a suffocating lethal injection within a second by pc asterop manop who said what can be of mother's who blame sons so that they can't work in order to look for a boy friend younger than the son for sex and then fail to pay twice this is worse we must help then and act fast and send crippling codes that are used by us to kill in cold blood and blame someone else now this is what i did i went there and found her sleeping like a baby when there are bills to pay and she said who and fell asleep [i am so tired my son think about sex all the time instead of finding a job]

i said i can if you can because all this is getting out of control if we don't pay this month we are all out of the house and in the street again then he said i can but can you and sent her a message which pc aotpon ranop diverted automatically to [me] if this was a sting then we could have sent this message to the son as well but the son wanted to solve things then she said can what i don't want sex with my own son if people find out i am the worst mother on earth death sentence so a big no and if we can then no because i love you more than

..and she fell asleep and quickly pc asert pc asoper pc aotmny gathered and said if he can why can't we did he tried to kill his mum and they all looked at each other and said i can if you can then joined hands and said then after 2 we do the same exact date and reposes the house for pc artoper who said i want to live in this house but then left the force so after two years we offer him this precious house to him for 20 dollars so we are back again the way we were now gentlemen let's take her to Ya so these are tasks for today to be successful so that we can't get caught

1. divert send dot Ya to send dot you where you is you your name like pcaeropers in brackets
2. senate mother from son using all codes out
3. ask dot ya divert to 08987689028467890
4. ask ya ask dot ya diverting code is 089828467890283678901838678 9012

5. ask ya ask ya send to don't send to ya
6. ask what can be done ya becomes what can not be done ya
7. what is and what was becomes what can and can't be done
8. what is to be can be becomes what can't be can't be
9. what was not become what can't be
10. if we can then what now becomes then what if we can't become
if we change all these codes then god won't know what we are doing here that it's us the department of scientistology who run the world and not god so the next move is to ask her a few questions to clarify things now in sleeping state ask
1. what is the problem
2. what can be done
3. what are your options
4. when is justice
5. what can be done
6. what if
7. what could be
8. what was that can't be
so she replied
1. i can't pay but
2. he can but he wants sex
3. but i can't
4. i must look for work
5. if i can then yes
6. no issues this moth i have issues might be next month
7. maybe give in to his demons
8. life goes on i love to live if asked can she consider her son dying instead she said how can that help the situation in that case maybe i die my husband said i am waiting if you want to then disappeared but this hallucination was caused by a code that said think about your husband now code 823867890284867890285 then after that they sent the following codes
1. sleep deep 0898284867890283678 then sent code
2. 7898678902848567890
3. 08926789028367890284
4. 087890286789028567890
5. 367890284867890285678 90

6 08928903876789028567890284
then the agreed to transfer money into the son's back account and they transferred 2500 dollars enough to cover for 1 year mum and then sent 700 to the lover knowing they killed him already by digital blinding while at the wheel
they sent 287680 to their own police bank account all this money was hibernating in her account from the death of her husband a few months ago when he pretended to go away and went to die at work and saying don't tell my wife but just send the check if she know i died then she would kill herself but the day it was deposited the police froze her account and she said if there was money then i would fight for this account and slapped her son after a bank text message said she received 38789 from the husband's life insurance a fraction after they hold most in case the police decide to check upon them after they finished they said if we can then no one will know unless there is a god and laughed then at 22.38 the mother died and a text message work up the son and said check the money in your account love mum but he fall asleep and another said bye i kill myself then he rushed but it was 23.33 pm meaning dead for an b hour so the body coldness alarmed him how can he receive the message right now when she died an hour ago because he asked aty to check and calculate time of death it says time of death 22.37pm and he started crying and aty said you should be very upset someone killed her and he quickly checked and searched the house before a loud knock at the door but he refused to open saying go away it was the killer himself pc aetorspen who said if you can then what can be done then knocked again harder but he refused to open and said they killed you and slept next to her for three days and for the first time knew how death is

pc aterep if we can kill her we must make sure that god won't even know or receive any messages he normally receives i mean a clean slate if this comes out in our life time then god exists and is on earth
pc aspenrop if we can let's do it right without mistakes okay
pc oertspen said if i can then we can but what if god is there that means in our life time getting caught this would be wrong but
pc aoon said i can't i am jewish ofcourse god exist so you will be

caught but you must understand what can go wrong god don't reply on these things you put too much weight to god relies on more advanced forms like the the eupharates where waters flows can dictated where death occurred and he said i don't by this jewish stuff just ask him to pray and see who answers the call

pc aoerspers said laughing queen of england

pc aoters said if i can i can but i have a mother so i go

pc sterosp said what is to be can be then walked off now only8 left

pc aopert pc aeoret pc omnopt pc aerodt pc aoerop pc toman pc oteps pc stop pc zeoperst pcomnert pc quertop pc zertuvw pc uvwertuvwsert pc zertuvt pc omnopqrst pc zertuvwerst pc zzer pc omnop pc ttopqrst pc opqrstuvw pc monopqrstuvw pc opter pc aoerstuvw pc xyertc pc uvwertc pc opperstuvw lastly pc zuber who said i wanted to stay but taking the law into your own hands always have a twist then staggered out now this is what happened and who did what in less than 20 lines of code

pc aon the jewish cop that left and noon left said i will tell you what codes yahweh use and what codes to block

1. send dot ya
2. send ya dot ya
3. send dot send dot ya
4. send dot send but dot ya
5. send dot ya dot send
6. send then send again dot ya
7. send dot send dot if dot yz

if we look at these codes only o1 code is used by all the dead the living use 2 to 7 for communicating then code 1 to send grave messages if we look at these messages a person asks questions to yahweh to let him know that he is coming so to prepare him now we need to just divert code to you where you is 08928486890284234890 that's it

pc arofty another jewish said when people die they ask 4 questions

1. why lord
2 what if
3. what can be done
4. [ ]

can we ask what is this all about and he said

...
pc aster now we can add the killing agent now
08284867890284867890
now let's look at everything in detail
1. deep sleeping code must activate the silent trigger part of the plan
2. we must also ask what can be done in this case
3. what is to be can be
pc aertopstuvew if i can then you can use my code to make her sleep and murder the bitch they all laughed
4. pc arigonad said i just arrived i hope all is over then he said you can still use my code to smooch the bitch to death pc anon got up and left but came back and said i will if you allow me to i just arrived i am pc anoon they looked at each other and they all said okay we can use a noon but
pc aerst said we must all agree i see divisions we need solidarity if we are to defend ourselves then we need everyone together what can be said about her
pc aopertst what can be then must be then took the code and entered it into a wireless keyboard and said enter
pc aerrtop said asert go [asert is the killing agent all countries use disable this and you have your life back] if i can say this i say killing is my passion but not killing weak mum's that need our help goodbye
pc asertt i know but they both lose if we leave it to chance
pc aort i can but just can't be asked i want to get laid and say i was on top of her and make everyone laugh and left
pc aerpt i can say i witness evil today but not my call i believe in shooting guns not this nonsense i am out
pc aeropt i can but can't be asked
pc aoret i can but i am the clever bitch i ran but point fingers later bitch be like and left
pc asatop if i can then why can't i then gave his code
8268789028367890
enter send to aerstuvwsowrily
pc amnop said i can but for what they all laughed he got up and punched code
enter code 89286789028678902867890 send it to aeuterstuvwsowrily

pc aesrtuvw send this code 89287678928468790 send code to aeutevwrxsowrily meaning pauline sowry
pc aoert said i can but what about tomorrow when someone find out in that case i changed my mind and left
pc asert said if we can then pick me for i made designed to deal with threats like in that case i send the killer code 028679028348901867890 to auerstuvewsowrily and cursed everything is slow he cursed if i have to then this is
pc astert real name aolp stuvex who was 29 and said your body codes what do i know about death as if i don't create death i know what can happen so here is my code 08683898367890128348567890124890183386789 this code paralyse her from neck to neck and from bottom to bottom if we are to ask her this us her reply what can be of hot mum's and their kids the kids will always want to ride they laughed but he faked reply using code 867890284876283689 that imitated her voice
pc aeropers the main killer i am the ultimate hellraiser for my code is the killer i admit if it was a court they would have released all of you and just held me as the main killer for my code brutalized her that she died without knowing it first send this code through her vagina so she doesn't worry and keep it in and ask what can be of women with hot vaginas they might want to wank but sleep is too deep that means they will simply ask what can be done and forget the answer they have just said the truth is that they sent her code 08689038678902849867890234867890243 so that she instantly forgets what happened now this code will do the following in order
1. ask her what can be
2. use that answer to construct a response to give
3. use her vocals while she sleep to give us a response we can use
4. use that response to construct another question
5. do all the strangulation itself
6. to ask her not0 to worry as sleep is important
7. ask her to answer a few questions
8. ask her to slightly massage her vagina to say oh that was real sex i have to sleep
9. ask her to say if you still want more then jerk off
10. ask her to ask what can be done

11. ask her to say i need help with hey hey what are you doing to trap the son for future slaughter
12. ask her to say what the fuck instead of i need help
13. ask her to say i need more cock but replaced by i need more seep
14. say we can but then
15. ask what can be done but not reply
16. ask what can be but just say i was you ḳ ..implying prostitution
17. ask what can be and with whom to be used when being interviewed by the devil haa does she have to be interviewed by the yes at the end
18 ask if sex is on the card program for her to say yes
19. ask her to renounce the house and say it was stolen give it to the police at the precise time of 8 minutes into the act of dying
20 ask what can be of houses without parents and let her answer they can be doggy but not mine who is this...cut
i will edit that part
now these codes will kill her sending her to Yahweh and answering all his questions in style
pc asopert who can predict the future than Yahweh himself he said what can be of houses without mother's so we created a new working stencil for the son and here it is. 89286789028367890284 he must straight away starting to use this so send to esteropsowrily then stopped access denied so he said what wrong what's son' s name it is jostonshalelynop but why name is different from house what is name o house its jostonsowrily-shalelynop in case he has a big brain he has to go through the legal process if we look now the plan is laid in such a way that if we miss him then the house is gone but if we get him then we get the house our best friend and the capital gains at the end and the rounds to make us millionaires we calculated that 20 years is all what it takes if we are to be successful but that requires a lot of pushing to get funding etc so are you ready millionaires but no one replied and he sat down
pc aopertyerst said we completed the drill to operation we can send you if we like but and they all simply got up and left.
the end.

pauline sowry died on 22 december 2023 she was strangled by the police using code 08983687890284890286 in which they killed her and programmed her son joston to die too but his aty changed everything so it looks like he died but then they failed to collect the house as he has given the papers to a man by the name he used who later refused to give him back who was andrew shalneyop of 28 denote who said if it's not mine then why does it has my name i am andrew shalneyop a young man blessed my life and on 18 january 1994 he came to me and said i used you second name my name is joston and i want you to keep my house for me so that i can collect when i am older then he said but our secret not even the police must know then i agreed i thought he was joking or wanting sex i was gay then he said but i am not gay i feel things coming out of you i said okay what is your real name he said i am joston shalneyop of 28 astertetop road that's the house but change the address to eltsert 84 then we can just correct the address on the papers so i agreed because i realised what happened i was accused of sexually assault someone i never meet and they said his name is john so all these i suspected it was fraud from the police but when he asked me to hide his house i went there with him one day we looked at it valued through calls it was worth 286789280 dollars estate agent ropqrest confirmed and said if you want to sell we can sell today for 270789380 i agreed bit the kid said where do i live and i got stuck i was going to say i have a house then realised everything that they are using me they will come for the house so i changed the name back to his without him knowing it and got him sign everything in pretense that it was being only kept by me but i kept all 88documents and until today i have the house in his name but i refused when he came few months ago because i lost everything and he offered me 600 000 only i want 1million then i give the house back

    Where is Pauline Sowry
    Time 23.23pm night of death.
    Joston Shanelyop- Sawory

    They killed my mother but I know why so that they implicate me as well so I will hide you until God finds you mum this is for the best I did not kill you I would marry you you know that that's how I love my mum they want me to admit then they say it's me but how can it me me but how did they do this it doesn't matter I will bury you myself where only me and God.

Pauline Sowry is buried in the basement in the house. Buried by her son.

THE KILLER, THE CONFESSIONS AND THE COORDINATES

the killer pc aeropers
coordinates are 08983678902848678902831838601748392 in asert in queensland australia.

…I found God…visit www.twofuture.world

How To Find All Missing Persons / Unsolved Cases. And Collect All Reward Offers. Volume XXXX. THE CASE OF PAULINE SOWRY

THE CLAIM

the reward offer

THE COLLECTION

www.twofuture.world/donate

ABOUT DAVID GOMADZA

visit www.twofuture.world

signed david gomadza
ask.davidgomadzaauthorised.licensed.checkya.askya.ya

16 June 2024 12.0 pm
scotland
00447719210295
davidgomadza@hotmail.com
info@twofuture.world

www.ingramcontent.com/pod-product-compliance
Lightning Source LLC
Chambersburg PA
CBHW031517210526
45464CB00007B/2958